Teaching
BITES

Inspiration for Teachers Everywhere

MARY MOODY FOSTER

Table of Contents

Preface

The stories in this little book are inspired by true events. I've changed the names of people and places and combined some stories. In a few cases, I omitted graphic language or disturbing events. For some readers, the stories will feel familiar. But if you've never taught in dilapidated schools or worked with impoverished students, some of the stories may seem surreal. I lived through all of it.

Some students and teachers may recognize themselves in these stories. The students have long since grown up, and some of the teachers have passed away. I have carried these students and our stories in my heart for decades. They resound with age-old human behavior and truths about children everywhere.

Kids have changed very little. But our culture has changed, often for the better. Many of the things we did are not tolerated today, from spankings to giving students a ride home. I have taught in private Christian schools and public schools, and in grade levels from elementary and middle to high school. The last six years of my teaching, I worked with gifted students and taught teachers how to teach gifted students. If you can dream up a wild, imaginative story of classroom shenanigans, it has actually happened somewhere in a school.

I'd like to thank my husband, Jim Foster, for being patient when I skipped meals and was in such a writer's Twilight Zone that he couldn't reach me. I would also like to thank my daughter, Mary

Beth, for giving up time out of her busy life to edit. She, along with my sons, Ed and Paul, cheered me on and supported this effort from the beginning. Each of my grandchildren had a part in making these stories come to life. Thank you Lyle, Yesica, Daveed, Guy, Kendall, Kate, Luke, Collyn, Brooks and Ellie for your inspiration.

Terrifying Stunts

Decades ago teachers didn't have to worry about their photos popping up on social media. We did crazy things for the school, some of it funny and some of it embarrassing. For a dinner theatre fundraiser, I once blackened two of my front teeth and accompanied myself on the piano as I sang Carol King's song "You've Got a Friend" to a co-worker. He dressed like a carpenter, wearing an impressive tool belt. He had cue cards that only the audience of parents could see. I sang, "You just call out my name, and you know wherever I am, I'll come running...to see you again." His cards echoed the words of the song with such phrases as: I wouldn't call out your name if I were drowning; and, I'd run away from you. Astonished at our audacity, Principal Pete wrapped up the show by saying, "And these people teach your children."

A popular school fundraiser is the magazine sale. I dread the extra work. But the school needs the money. Principal Pete asks three of us teachers to help with the big promotional event. In the gym after lunch, the students are rowdy with high anticipation and ready to riot. The magazine people take us volunteers aside to show us our costumes, which resemble space suits. I am not paying attention. A crucial mistake.

I pay attention to my class in the bleachers and ask my friend Jane to watch them. I hurry back to the platform, a portable stage about five feet high. Someone helps me into the heavy, giant suit and I climb the steps. At the top I have to jump over a one-foot gap between the steps and the stage. The suit is cumbersome and causes me to trip. One leg gets wedged down in the gap. I yell for help. Though I'm a small woman, it takes two people to pull me out. They strain and heave. This should be a clue that things will not be normal. Frustrated and anxious, I see the others have started the performance. I join them and try to catch up. I don't understand. Suddenly my friend Sissy, a tiny delicate lady, sprints toward the back of the stage in a mad dash, leaps high and lands on a giant velcro wall. What? And there she stays. Stuck. The kids are in hysterics.

I say to Rick, the other teacher, "I don't think I ought to do that." Ignoring me, he charges to the wall and smashes his entire body into it. Stuck high up there. The kids scream in absolute spasms. He can't move his head, which is turned grotesquely to one side. Like a trapped character in a crime film, he rolls his eyes to try and see behind him. Both teachers are stuck about four feet up on this incredible wall. They yell at me, "You can do it! Come on!"

Now let's think this through. I am a teacher. I am a teacher with all the honor and dignity that go with that title. Pleading, I look at Principal Pete who laughs and signals for me to GO. The students yell, "GO! GO! GO!" The magazine person yells, "It's for the KIDS!" I burst forward as hard as I can, bounce off the stage and catapult myself against the wall. Stuck. We laugh and cheer. They slap me on the back. I am a teacher.

As cheers swell to dangerous decibels, we leave the stage and peel out of our jumpsuits. Embarrassed, I hand my suit to the magazine person and whisper, "You'll need to wash this one."

**Colossians 3:23 Whatever you do,
work at it with all your heart,
as working for the Lord.**

*Lord, thank you for fun and laughter.
Thank you for giving me joy in doing new things.
Please keep helping me do all these challenging things.*

Clandestine

Flashback to my very first day of teaching. I am gulping the intoxicating drink of power. I'm delivering my first lesson to expectant students. They're nodding and agreeing, looking at my syllabus and taking notes. Though their excitement is gone by the end of class period, I don't notice. It's all exciting for me. I am THE teacher.

At the end of my first week, I bring home three books to scour for the next week of English classes. I have 155 students, grades 9, 10 and 11, with varying levels of ability. And I'm still excited. I also have many test papers to grade. But I feel good. I've done some excellent planning. Heaving the load, I stumble to my car. One week completed.

By October I am staying up late at night to do school work. I cry in the shower each morning because I don't have a clue how to manage it all. When I reach the school, I struggle with my load of books, coffee thermos, lunch bag and purse. A fellow teacher eyes my burden with a chuckle. I breathe a quick prayer for God to help me through the day. Suddenly a student crashes into me. She's running from a boy. He dips and ducks out of sight. Her books fly. My myriad belongings land with a painful crush on my feet. In an angry voice I accost her, "What are you doing? Don't you know you can't run in the hall?" Proud teacher.

Seasoned teachers urge me to fly by the seat of my pants in moments when all else fails. They laugh and say, "Startle them! Tell them to look at that mouse squeezing under the door. Segue from there." Another clever method they teach me is to let students check each other's tests. But I catch Bee doctoring her classmate's tests to look like an A. When I give her the stink eye, she quips, "You don't look at the papers anyway." Who's busted now?

I become clandestine in my effort to manage classes. I call rabble-rouser Raylene outside the room and say, "I'm asking you to do this because I think I can trust you." I hand her a note addressed to my friend Diane. Raylene can clearly read this. The note says: *Mrs. Clark, I have a list of five students that I believe I can trust.* That's all it says. No names are on the note. This is my effort at the power of suggestion.

My friend Diane and I had arranged a plan in advance for Raylene to deliver my cryptic message to her. Raylene becomes my best ally. Whenever a student is disrespectful, Raylene calls out, "Don't talk to Mrs. F that way." Raylene volunteers for many errands. I finally learn to work smarter, although that is an ongoing effort. I rarely take anything home, and I leave the coffee thermos behind. The cafeteria food now tastes delicious. I have no idea how all this translates into a Zoom lesson during COVID times. God bless those zooming teachers.

Matthew 6:33 But seek first His kingdom and His righteousness, and all these thing will be given to you as well.

Lord, help me through each day.
Give me a triple portion of wisdom to work smarter.

You Never Know

During my class free period the guidance counselor calls me to a meeting about a 7th grader named Josh, a 15-year-old who is supporting his family. Last week he showed me a large wad of cash. I feared it was drug money. When I asked him about it, he said he had a job after school until 10 at night. That explains why he often falls asleep in class.

At the meeting we learn that his mother has cancer. His dad is a long-distance truck driver, gone for weeks at a time. Josh says his dad won't give his mom any money. They don't have food if he doesn't bring money home. The guidance counselor calls Child Protective Services.

When I get back from the meeting, the students are coming into the classroom. Judy tries to lift a decorative apple from my desk. My students love to touch these trinkets. At first I don't mind, but after they break a few of these cute little things that students like to bring to the teacher, I want to protect these items. First I put a sign on the front of the desk that says, "If you can read this, you're too close." But that is not very polite. So I put sticky-tack under each novelty to make it difficult to lift or knock off the desk. We teachers love sticky-tack so much that we'd sticky-tack our grandmas if we could. I wish protecting our students were that simple.

While I chuckle at the notion of trinkets plastered to my desk, I can't get my mind off Josh. He's a kid who meticulously sketches warships. Each unique design has a stunning high-powered weapon. He once proudly presented these sketches to the class. He was articulate and included a detailed explanation of how each operates. The details were astounding. Sadly, the police hauled his younger brother Wes away from school one afternoon. Josh was overwhelmed.

Wes had a meltdown in class. He turned over desks, flailed his arms, punched any kid he could reach, and finally ran headlong into the teacher sending her to the floor where she banged her head in a bloody injury. The teacher across the hall rushed to her rescue and another colleague followed. It was too much.

As the squad car pulled away with his brother, Josh ran screaming behind it. He turned and trudged back, but when he saw the principal and several teachers standing where his brother had been taken, he yelled, "You can't do this to my brother. I'll kill all of you!"

There is a good ending to this. No one was seriously hurt when Wes fell apart in class. Though the teacher's head bled in a scary stream, it did not require stitches. I don't know about Wes, but Josh later joined the Army. Last I heard, he was a very good soldier. Maybe they became his family.

Jeremiah 29:11 "For I know the plans I have for you," declares the Lord, "plans to prosper you and not to harm you, plans to give you hope and a future."

Lord, I claim this verse from Jeremiah for Josh and Wes. Make your plans clear to them both. Help them to prosper and not be harmed, to have hope and a bright future.

Wild Goose Chase

My class settles into their desks. It's 8 a.m. Suddenly Larry throws his books across the room and yells, "I don't have to do any work. I'm sick of school." He adds a few curse words for emphasis. I ask the students to start writing about the topic I've put on the board: What really bothers you?

I whisper to Larry to let's step outside a minute. It's crucial to keep his dignity. I close the door and ask whether he's taken his ADHD meds that morning. He answers that they ran out of it. His grandparents haven't gotten the prescription refilled. I know that his dad and mom are in prison for drugs, and his grandparents are doing their best. I'll have to call them.

The next day Larry is angry because I once again ask him to step outside to talk. I talk, and he talks. We both listen. All good. Seemingly. When he gets to his desk, he suddenly shouts to me, "I'll burn your house down!" He is my neighbor.

Sometimes these cases call for drastic or ridiculous measures. Telling him to stay a minute in the hall, I return to my desk and jot a few words on a sheet, fold it and staple it closed. I ask him to please take the note to the office. I have arranged earlier with the school secretary that when this student comes to the front office with a folded, stapled sheet and "WGC" written on the outside, she will ask him to take a seat and wait a few minutes. "WGC" stands for Wild Goose Chase. Being out of the hub of the classroom, he can calm down. I have now to calm myself down. A wise friend once told me to free myself. I'm trying to figure out how.

That Saturday my doorbell rings, and there stands Larry and his grandmother. She bellows with profound grandmother love, "Larry has something to say to you." He looks down at his shoes and whines, "I'm sorry."

She takes his arm and jiggles it to get his attention. "Try that again, Larry! And start with I'm sorry that..." He humbly complies, "I'm sorry that I said I would burn your house down."

On the last day of the school year, I give back to students the items I had to confiscate. The principal keeps these in the office until the parent comes to pick them up or until the last day of school. The students talk softly amongst themselves. As Larry walks from the classroom for the last time, he is friendly and happy. I recall that Larry always got along with his classmates, and they like him. I'm handing out the large, sealed envelopes with everything from water guns to tiny Strawberry Shortcake dolls to Mickey Mouse watches. The final school bell rings. Caught up in the gridlock of exuberant students, Larry smiles and calls over his shoulder, "You were always sending me on a Wild Goose Chase!"

Proverbs 6:5 Free yourself.

Lord, help me understand how to free myself
in a job that is very challenging.

Athletic talent

Jack is a good kid with learning disabilities, although he is in the mainstream classroom. When he reaches 7th grade, the girls begin to notice him. He's tall, good looking and athletic. And it helps that the football coach has recruited him to play the position of end. The coach looks at each player's grades at midterm and again at the end of the term. If a player is failing his grade, or he gets into trouble of any kind, he is kicked off the team.

I am passing out midterm reports. As everyone who has ever been a student knows, we send these reports home for parent signature. Jack has a midterm grade of 60 because he has not turned in any of his homework assignments. As soon as I get back to the front of the classroom, I engage a student in conversation and suddenly sense something very big, moving very fast around the back of the room and along the side wall. I jerk my head in that direction and see Jack running toward me. He drops down on his knees and slides the last eight feet to reach me. With praying hands he looks up at me in tears and says, "Please, please, please Mrs. F. Please don't make me take this grade home. My mom will make me quit the football team."

Now understand that this kid is in middle school. He should be caring very much about ridicule from the other students. But they are as stunned as I am. I must think quickly of a way to handle this to save his dignity. I say as slowly and as sincerely as I can, "Ok, Jack, let's talk after class. I'll take care of this."

In the end, I assign him extra work to bring his grade up to an 80. Being reasonable, I'm only giving him eight assignments. Do you know how many assignments it would actually take to raise a grade point average from 60 to 80? And this is how an Individual Education Plan helps exceptional students.

I run into Jack ten years later at the elementary school. We are happy to see each other. He tells me he is there to pick up his little boy in 1st grade. He speaks confidently, "I didn't fit in that school thing. I got me a girlfriend, and this little boy that I love."

Matthew 5:7 Blessed are the merciful, for they will be shown mercy.

Lord, Jack is a humble young man. Look to him with your mercy. Please watch over him so that no one can take advantage of him or harm him. Help him to be prosperous and happy all his life.

Changing the world

Linda, the new teacher across the hall, looks very confident. She is polite and calm with the students. I have been apprehensive about a replacement for the previous teacher, Lily, who retired. She and I had worked very well together and were compatible. But I find myself pleased with Linda, and I think we will make a great team.

About three weeks into the school year, I hear a commotion in the hall. I open my room door and find Linda's students horse playing and running near the restroom at the end of the hall. Standing at her door, she watches them but makes no move to intervene. Students in her room are out of their desks in a free-for-all. Paper flies, water sprays, and students shout and spar with each other. I ask Linda what's going on, and she replies calmly that she's giving them a bathroom break. I see this will only get worse. Diplomatically, I explain that the students can't be allowed as a group to visit the restroom. It's best to let them go one at a time. She is confident and assures me that they will be fine.

Next, Linda allows students to roam around the school. They have told her they need a break. I explain that the students are scamming her. She says kids can be trusted. But the chaos worsens, and all manner of problems arise. Suddenly without notice, Linda quits or is fired. I never knew what really happened. She came to me at the end of her last day to say goodbye. Though she had been a banker for years, Linda had always yearned to teach children. Needing a change because of burnout, she decided to try teaching. She wanted to make a difference. The saddest thing she said was, "I thought I could change the world."

Disappointment and disillusion left Linda with no desire ever to teach again. She was on a mission, but she needed more training.

2 Corinthians 4:9 We are...persecuted, but not abandoned; struck down, but not destroyed.

Lord, bless Linda and help her to find meaningful work,
to make a difference in the world. Look into her heart, Lord.
Please find her a career that will fulfill her.

Knowledge
Beyond Geography

The first job I land right out of college is teaching summer school to 10th graders who are required to retake English so they can move up to 11th grade. We are reading a story set in Pearl Harbor.

We are discussing what they like about the story. I am trained to ask questions according to each student's level of ability. Teachers are to choose one of these questions – what, when, where, why and how – based on the student's ability to respond. When I get to the question "Where is Pearl Harbor?" no one knows the answer. Finally after a long pause, I give a hint. It's on a beach at the ocean.

One hesitant, shy hand goes up and says, "Wilmington." My heart suddenly skips a beat because this is a pivotal moment. I could respond with sarcasm and ridicule, inciting a chain reaction of laughter from the rest of the class. This is where my training pays off and not only keeps order in the class, but also saves his dignity, which is what good teaching is all about.

"Thank you, Ray," I say with sincere kindness. "Actually Pearl Harbor is on the Pacific Ocean. Does anyone know where people sometimes wear grass skirts and do the hula dance?" Someone answers "Hawaii," but Ray doesn't know.

As we get to the end of the summer session, we begin to share personal experiences. Some are funny, but Helen's is tragic. She tells about her grandmother who had a sudden headache on a Friday, and the doctor said it was a brain tumor. She died the following Tuesday. At this point I consider putting a stop to the sad sharing, but the others are shifting in their desks with anticipation of telling their own stories. Though these are somewhat morbid, the students want to talk about it. They ask questions of each other and express sympathy.

Dylan describes the time he was riding a minibike through a series of dirt trails on his farm. He turned onto a side path unfamiliar to him. His neighbor saw this and ran screaming his name to stop him. Motoring full speed, he hit a metal cable that was strung across the path, and it nearly cut him in half at the waist. He was in the hospital a long time but made a miraculous recovery.

Ray says he had a twin brother who "fell in the fire," as he put it. He explained that they were toddlers, playing near the fireplace. His twin got too close to the fire and fell in. He died a few days later.

Teachers must take many required psychology courses, but textbook methods and real life situations are vastly different. There's a fine line between reacting with shock to stories and showing concern. As the saying goes, "Nothing prepared me for this."

John 13:34 ...Love one another. As I have loved you, so you must love one other.

Lord, there are many Rays in the world.
There is a strong pull in people's hearts to ridicule, to size
a person up and decide who they are and what they are about.
Teach us to love, to have compassion toward others.
For we are all deserving of love and respect.

She Hides It

Liz is a new student, arriving August 31. We've been in school since August 20. She seems just like all the other kids but blessedly quiet, a welcome relief in my large, unusually energetic class. This year I have an 8th grade class of forty kids. School law, or maybe a suggestion as you will soon see, requires a class limit of thirty-five. Principal Gaines tells me that the brass from the State Department of Education are coming to observe the school. He adds that we are not in compliance with class size, and it's not his fault, but he has a solution. When they arrive, he will announce over the intercom system that we have visitors in the building. I am then to immediately send five students to the library with work. By the skin of our teeth.

The curious thing about our new student Liz is that she never takes off her heavy jacket. Each time I mention it to her, she says she likes to wear her coat. The school has no air conditioner. Isn't she uncomfortable in the southern August heat? She says no.

Liz is so quiet that I barely know she's in the room. She has nothing to do with the other students. She keeps her head lowered most of the time, as if trying to be invisible. Hoping to draw her out, I stand near her desk sometimes and smile when she looks up. One day Liz lingers as the others leave class. I can tell she wants to talk. She mumbles casually, "You want to know why I really wear my coat all the time?" With great and careful effort, she peels off her coat to reveal raw lashes on her arms. This is not the time for me to act cool, but also not the time to seem shocked.

So I respond with a sad look of compassion. In a soft, slow voice, I ask, "What happened, Liz?" She tells me her dad beats her with an electric extension cord, especially if she makes a bad grade. I face her and say in my battle voice, "Oh Liz, I am so sorry. He should not hurt you like that." I have no training for this. But I do know one thing. I am required by law to report even a suspicion of abuse to the school social worker who contacts Child Protective Services.

The social worker calls Liz's aunt who lives in the next state. That day Liz is taken to her aunt's house where hopefully she will remain safe. None of us ever heard any more about Liz or what happened to her abusive father. But I did the right thing. She needed to tell someone, and it touched my heart that she chose me. I must have made her feel safe in my classroom. She must have known that I cared.

Isaiah 41:13 For I am the Lord, your God, who takes hold of your right hand and says to you, Do not fear; I will help you.

Lord, my friend and my helper, give me discernment so that I can tell when a student or a fellow teacher needs someone. Someone to tell. And watch over all the children. Stop the abuser, Lord. Hold back the hand that would cause harm.

That Hurts

My most enjoyable teaching experience is at a K-8 school in a rural farming community. Kids who grow up on a farm are not afraid of any creature, great or small. My 7th graders bring corn snakes and rat snakes to school—in the name of science or of inspiring poetry. These kids understand animals and plants and are beyond their years in this knowledge. To them the snakes are frisky or lazy. I grew up visiting my grandparents' farm in rural South Carolina, and although I love nature and God's creatures, I don't have these kids' gift for nature. Besides snakes, they proudly show us salamanders, baby pigs and goats, and even an old mule brought to the classroom window where he heehawed and goggled at us. He wasn't a happy mule.

On this particularly bright day, I am teaching a science lesson on water pollution by drawing a picture on the board. I draw a house and the ground beneath the house, water pipes and an aquifer. Suddenly a flash of something too green for human flesh is sneaking up behind me. I snap my head toward it, and there stands Lefon with a chameleon hanging from each of his earlobes like earrings. "Lefon, what is that?" I gasp and punch jabs in the air with my piece of chalk. He moans with an expression of pain on his face, "It hurts! It hurts!"

I now see that he is wearing living jewelry. The lizards don't seem able to disengage themselves. "Set them free, Lefon!" I growl. The class is shrieking with joy at this circus. I continue, "Class, get in your seats, we'll play the lizard game." Now this is an old trick. It's called teaching by the seat of your pants. I have no earthly idea what the lizard game will be, but I'm in just enough panic to think at superhuman speed.

I bark, "Get into two teams. We're having a question game." After they are settled, I begin pulling questions out of my brain, anything about lizards. Were dinosaurs giant lizards? Do lizards lay eggs? Then I switch the game to students asking questions. They come up with: How much does a lizard weigh? Can you eat lizard? Do you fry 'em?

I notice that Noah and Will are at the back of the room doing something at the work table. I tell them to join us. Noah laughs and asks me to come see their science experiment. I move to the table with brisk steps. These two are frozen in place, and they know.

I have no words as I stare at their work. Noah is holding down one of the lizards while Will traces an outline of him on a sheet of paper. Words flood from Noah's mouth, "And we could do this all over the walls and have a lizard wall. Oh and we could get your ink stamp and dip the lizards in it and stamp their shape on the walls— no!—mash 'em a little bit to get red from their blood." He and Will blast out a loud laugh.

I'm incensed but maintain a steely calm. Like a war drum I beat my words, "You two take those creatures, walk to the window, and set them free. No, no, I don't want to hear your case for keeping them. Take them now. And where is the other lizard?" Half of the class is saying YES set them free. The others are whining NO. Celia says, "I've named them Suki and Stark." I stand still and glare at them. They finally give in. Deborah cries, "Their family will be looking for them. They need to get back to their home." And that ends the debate.

Thankfully there are more of these days than days of sadness or trouble.

Genesis 2:19 Now the Lord God had formed out of the ground all the beasts of the field and all the birds of the air. He brought them to the man to see what he would name them; and whatever the man called each living creature, that was its name.

Lord, I thank you for the students who make our school day fun and interesting. Bless the children who love your creation and who help take care of it.

Confiding

High school teachers face very different challenges. Though I would prefer not to be told, teenagers often share things that are private and personal. It's difficult not to react to the sad or scary things they tell us. Patricia comes to me one day during my planning period. She is not one of my students but wants to chat. It seems that she has casually dropped by for a visit. But in no time she is breathlessly telling me that her mom and dad are fighting all the time, and she has moved in with her boyfriend and his parents.

"What do you think I should do?" she asks suddenly in a pleading voice. My muscles tense because this is not advice I should be giving. I know enough about counseling to say "How do you feel about this?" My heart pounds. I don't want to go against her parents' authority, and I also know that teenagers often distort the true situation. But she needs someone to listen, so I do.

Patricia is worried about what will happen to her little sister, Kari. She speaks with a pained expression when she describes how their mom got so angry with Kari that she pressed her leg with the hot iron, which left the iron imprint. She smiles and adds, "But it's almost healed up." I frown strongly, but I am crying inside. I will do something about this. She asks me to promise not to tell her parents. I listen but don't give advice. She seems content with this and finishes by saying she is leaving school early. With that said, I let her go but I hurry straight to the guidance counselor, who immediately picks up the phone to call Child Protective Services.

It turns out Patricia's parents are fighting violently. Patricia is a senior, and two days after we have talked, she and her boyfriend run away together. The other students say they got married. At 4 p.m. several days later, Patricia and her husband, Mike, stop by my classroom. This feels awkward. I smile at them as they stand in the doorway. In a forced cheery and friendly voice I offer, "Come in!" But inside I am overwhelmed with the feeling that this is not the best decision for them. But they are married. What can I do but say something nice?

Patricia describes their new life. They are living with Mike's parents. He's working with his dad in farming. Patricia is looking for a job in a store. I tell them that I am sure they will be fine and that Patricia will get a job in no time. She proudly shows me her diamond and gold band and sheepishly explains, "We got it dirt cheap at a discount store." I reply that it's not about the jewelry or how much it costs or where it comes from.

I pray often for those two kids. And I'm not judging. I married at 18. With the prayers of family and friends, I'm still married to the same man. People have been marrying too young since the beginning of time.

John 16:33 I have told you these things, so that in me you may have peace. In this world you will have trouble. But take heart I have overcome the world.

Lord, help our students to know that they have choices and help me to teach them how to choose wisely. Provide what they need. Help me to have the courage to be available to students when they need to talk.

Going Up

Chevy is a 6th grader who doesn't mean to be mischievous. He is busy. He is likeable and entertaining. Two events stand out with Chevy. The first concerns science projects. Chevy wants to do a diorama about snakes. He owns a corn snake he named Squeeze. He loves his corn snake. Recently, builders came to his house to remodel a bathroom, and they happened upon Chevy's corn snake wrapped around the base of the toilet. They refused to work unless someone removed the snake.

Chevy told them this was Squeeze's favorite hangout. As they talked, Squeeze silently escaped into the toilet water. "It's OK," he tells the workmen. "I can just scoop him out." As Chevy reaches into the toilet for his pet, the workers jump back. During their work the rest of that day, they talk incessantly about the boy who scooped the snake out of the toilet water. And named that thing Squeeze. You could hear them laugh down the street.

For his science project I give clear instructions that Chevy is allowed to cut pictures only from certain books. I hand Chevy my *Field Guide to Reptiles* and say, "You may not cut anything from this book. Look at the cover. No cutting. Right?"

He answers, "No cutting, ma'am."

For an overly energetic kid, Chevy has one of the best projects of all, his laser focus a result of his passion for snakes. It isn't until July that I make a surprising discovery. While trying to identify a snake in my yard, I detect a missing picture from my beloved *Field Guide to Reptiles*. Live and learn, as the saying goes. This loss of a photo is my tuition into the knowledge that if it is valuable, do not let kids use it. And by all means do not even mention the word *cut*.

The second thing with Chevy is over the top. And I do mean the top. As we walk back to class after a program in the gym, a student comes jogging up to me and stammers that Chevy is missing. What next with this wild child? A crowd gathers and gestures up to the sky. I realize now that I am the last one to know it. No, he has not been translated like Elijah in the Bible. Chevy is on the roof of the gym. I scream, "Come down, Chevy! I'm calling your mom right now!"

But Chevy is enjoying the audience below. The kids are all pointing up and yelling, "Hey Chevy! You gonna jump?" This eggs him on. He grins his brilliant, contagious grin and starts to sway his hips and take dance steps back and forth, clearly showing off. The students suddenly have some rhythm in their heads that moves them to clap a beat, which only encourages Chevy.

He is full out dancing now. No fear. I tearfully pray he doesn't fall. But like a circus actor, he actually takes a bow as if on a stage and shimmies down at top speed. I could be in big trouble for this. I ponder what to do. What would Jesus do? It's been estimated that teachers make 1,500 decisions a day. Decision fatigue. We need God's help for that.

I know one of the builders who was at Chevy's house to remodel the bathroom, over 20 years ago. I run into him in a hardware store one day. Tom and I laugh at the memory of Chevy scooping his snake Squeeze from the toilet. I share the story about Chevy dancing on the roof of the gym. Tom replies, "Did you know he graduated from the Air Force Academy and is a pilot today with Southwest Airlines?"

Struggling to talk while strangling on laughter, I tell Tom, "Chevy said he climbed on the roof that day to scoop out his ball from the hole."

John 14:27 Peace I leave with you; my peace I give you. I do not give to you as the world gives. Do not let your hearts be troubled, and do not be afraid.

Lord, help me to make good decisions in my school day.
And when a student gets so out of control that
I am unable to do any good, please take control.

Spies Watching

In the hall my teammates and I discuss the thing we fear. The computer. It is 1984. The computer is here. At the first training session, I puzzle over it. The nervous instructor begins, "There are three steps to starting. You will mash two buttons. You can't just mash them any old way. You have to mash them in order. Now everybody stand up. Now mash the button on top of the monitor. The monitor is the TV screen. As you start to sit down, mash the button on the biggest machine, your hard drive. You will enter the computer by way of MS-DOS." I think to myself, isn't a hard drive an exhausting trip in the car in blinding rain?"

Even after our training session, we are all clueless and fearful. Betty declares, "I'm not using that machine. Never gonna happen! I would break it first thing, and they'd fire me." To this day Betty has kept her vow. Older, seasoned teachers who have soldiered through beyond age 65 are now retiring. The rest of us muddle through and shed tears of frustration. Fear shoots through all of us with the paralyzing virus of misconception. Not five minutes into my first time in the computer lab, the hard drive begins to whir and grind as if dying. I shout, "I'm sorry! I'm so sorry! I broke it!"

One day as I am typing a syllabus for a Julius Caesar study, my perfect document disappears in a flash. My heart and brain flood with anguish. I grit my teeth and scowl, "This stupid machine has eaten my syllabus. The screen jumps here and there. It has a mind of its own." My friend Louise vows that her computer watches everything she does. I ask her how she knows that.

She looks warily around the lab and whispers, "You know the government has been spying on us forever, and now with computers they can be even sneakier. I was watching my show the other night and eating some chips when a man came on the TV and told me to eat more chips." She continues, "Then one night a woman came on an ad and said, 'You are already using this soap. You know you want to use the new soap with mint fragrance.' And that's the soap I use!"

One day I discover that I can master this intimidating machine. I happen to pass by the computer room where 25 students are studying their screens. I am impressed with their level of focus. Pure absorption. In that moment I know that if they can do it, surely I can. I ask the students what they are doing, and they tell me they are painting pictures and playing Oregon Trail. I am astonished!

As I learn more about the computer, I am delighted to discover the floppy disc. With it I can work on documents anywhere I find a computer. Put the disc in the hard drive, follow directions on the monitor to find the file, and continue my work. Save it only to the floppy disc. My only problem is the occasional embarrassment of using a computer term incorrectly, such as calling the disc a flabby disc. I must have connected floppy with flabby skin. I'm sure I provided wonderful comic entertainment for my computer savvy coworkers.

Incidentally, the Oregon Trail game was created in 1971 to teach history about the pioneers. It's still around today, only new and improved.

Hebrews 13:8 Jesus Christ is the same yesterday and today and forever.

Lord, I can't do this alone. Change is hard. It's all moving too fast. Come and make yourself real to me while I try to complete this work.

Then There Was 9-11

On September 11, 2001, when terrorists are bombing the World Trade Centers and the Pentagon, I am teaching 7th grade. A fellow teacher, whose husband works on the nearby Air Force Base, comes to my classroom door and pulls me out to tell me, "We're under attack. They know of four planes so far but they fear more. The base is on alert." Minutes later the assistant principal stops by and whispers, "Do not turn on your TV. The kids do not need to see this." The 8th grade classes are watching it in real time.

By lunchtime most of the students have heard about the suicide bombers. Parents come early to pick up many of them. My afternoon students are very frightened. I let them ask questions, and we talk about it the entire class period. I can't consider giving them any work because they need to talk.

I assure them in my fighting voice, "Listen to me. Those people don't want anything we have out here on our farms. We're waaaay out here in the country. They're not interested in our cows and chickens. We're safe here. They want banks and government buildings in huge cities like New York. So you're safe out here in the country. And you better believe that we have the best military fighting force in the entire world." Some of their parents are Air Force pilots.

I don't know for sure what is going on with all those planes, but my nervous, tearful students need to calm down. They need assurance that everything will be alright. We don't even know whether there might be a huge fleet of planes or ships from a foreign enemy.

My mother tells me later that a distant cousin of mine, a general no less, who works in the Pentagon, has a miracle story to tell. We'll call her Sue. Sue is having new carpet installed in her home on September 11. The workers call her several times before 8:30 that morning about the installation. After so many calls, Sue tells the people in her office that she needs to go home and see that the job is done right. Shortly after that, terrorists bomb the Pentagon. Her desk is located in the area that was destroyed.

The following week I speak with 15-year-old Mark, one of my 7th grade boys who struggles with school. We're in the hall and I see that he is gathering everything from his locker. He says in a voice of concern, "You won't see me after today. I'm going to join the army. They need me. They need more soldiers to protect America. I'm going to learn all about guns, even machine guns and bombs. Tell everybody that I'm going to fight. They'll see me when I get back."

He truly believes he can do this. I think it best not to discourage him; not to tell him that he is not legally old enough to join the military. I simply nod to him and reply, "I hope you will be able to help. But if they have enough soldiers, maybe you can come back to school. We'll miss you, Mark."

Romans 14:8 If we live, we live to the Lord; and if we die, we die to the Lord. So, whether we live or die, we belong to the Lord.

Lord, there are many people who have lost loved ones in a senseless, violent attack. They are still suffering. Comfort them. Help us to have peace.

It Is Rocket Science

In a 5th grade science class, we are learning about planes and flight, the four forces of lift, gravity, thrust and drag. My student Chad suggests he can bring his rocket-building kits. I let him bring his three kits—two small rockets and a very large three-foot rocket. As the class discusses and sketches what they think the four forces are, Chad begins to build.

He spreads out his large sheet of directions. Though he tends to be talkative and mischievous, he is now quiet. The class focuses on Chad and asks what he plans to do with the rockets. I am thinking of a table in the back of the room with a rocket display. To lessen class distraction, I soon put him in the hallway to work. A window on my door allows me to juggle the class and his work. I check in with him often. I offer him a table and chair, but he prefers to work on the floor. He works on the rockets about forty minutes each day.

A week later as he finishes painting black rings and placing USA stickers on the rockets, he tells me about the engine, the electric igniter, how the flame burns through the propellant. He asks, "Can I launch 'em here at school?"

"Are you kidding? No way is that going to happen!" I exclaim. But Lord help me, that little smarty talks me into it. He makes a solid case. Everybody in the school can come out and watch. He has orange cones to keep people back at a safe distance. When the principal expresses concern, Chad also talks him into it. Future U.S. President?

The crowd gathers outside as Chad places his rockets and cones. Then Chad of the Fifth Grade addresses the crowd with an introduction. I am stunned. Chad explains that the principles behind launching a big rocket or a small rocket are the same. His voice gets stronger and more confident as he adds, "Even if you're setting off a model rocket or launching a giant rocket to Mars, it's the same." The crowd is impressed and responds with ooh and aah. He continues, "The old launches were by chance. So if you set off a rocket, it could go anywhere. Do anything. They might skitter around, shoot sparks and explode in the air. But they're good to go now." He has researched rocket science.

I'm getting very apprehensive. Have I made a crucial mistake in allowing Chad to do this? The principal sternly warns that the rockets had better land on school property. That's the big problem. Landing. Chad lights the first fuse. The little rocket soars and lands nicely on the school grounds. The crowd screams with joy. The next little rocket does the same. The buildup to the big rocket is almost too much for the kids. They clap and scream, "GO! GO! GO!" The students standing next to me are shivering with excitement and fear.

As Chad lights the big fuse, it makes an ominous whoosh and thrusts upward with a lot more fire than the others. We don't see it for a few seconds. Dear Lord, let it land safely away from people and property. We don't see it until it lands on a nearby house. My heart beats like a war drum. The flames burn on. I yell, "Quick! Call the fire department!"

Chad proclaims, "No ma'am! I got this!"

Now why would I ever believe that a 5th grader has "Got this?" A rocket launch! Fire! But parents and school leaders are impressed. Maybe not the principal. (If you're curious, the fire went out in seconds on its own.) As I drive from the school at four in the afternoon, I park my car in front of the house where the rocket landed. I look up at the roof for any charred spots. I don't see any.

**Joshua 1:9 Have I not commanded you?
Be strong and courageous. Do not be terrified;
do not be discouraged, for the Lord your God
will be with you wherever you go.**

*Lord, you are the God of the heavens.
You guide us. Help us to trust you more, for our safety,
our food, our home, and our families. I believe that one day we
will fly to our home with you above.*

Tape on Her Mouth

Just when you think you understand kids, you've got the teaching degree, you've earned the certificate, you find yourself at a loss to help. In my 6th grade class, students are enjoying rifling through a box of curtain panels, cloth remnants from my sewing bag, hats, belts, sashes, old wrist corsages, anything for a costume to act out poetry or a story passage. Yes, I saved all these things for such a time as this. They find purple satin for a queen, green for a forest creature, red velvet for a soldier. Whatever they want, it can be. The students talk and exclaim pleasantly.

Casey is at my desk, and I ask her to come back to the costume box. She tells me she needs tape. I watch as she goes back to her desk and does—what? She tapes her mouth shut. Her face reddens. Her friend Brooks runs over to her and rips off the tape. Casey lets out a scream. I rush to her and whisper, "What's going on?" She won't say a word. Brooks tells me that Casey can't breathe through her nose and is to have surgery the following week. When I ask Casey why she taped her mouth, she is silent and won't look at me.

I find a book on costumes for her. As I cross the room to take Casey the book, I am distracted by Ryan and Sam, practicing Shakespeare flourishes by waving their arms and throwing their heads up in a regal gesture. I love their enthusiasm. Both are clad heavily in royal blue and gold fabric draped and wound smartly over their clothes. I ask them which story they chose.

"Prometheus the Fire-Bringer!" exclaims Sam. "Have you got any makeup we can put on?" Ryan hollers back, "Nooooo! No makeup!" I tell them I have no makeup but wouldn't let them use it if I did. Almost as a chorus several others ask, "Why? We need stage makeup!"

"Germs!" I shoot back.

In a sudden burst Ryan bellows, "Maybe we could figure out something for a real fire." At this, I give him such a stink eye that he literally shrinks behind the cobbled-together "dressing room" curtain.

I finally get to Casey with the costume book. She sneers at it. I find a photo of a white Roman toga draped with a swatch of scarlet fabric. "Take a look at this! Isn't it beautiful?" I say cheerily. Slowly she turns around, her back to me now. She doesn't want any of this. I turn to help Cathy with a belt I've brought from home. It's an old 1950s accessory of my mother's. Brooks taps me on the shoulder and gestures toward Casey. She has again plastered masking tape on her mouth. I ask Brooks to please go pull off the tape and then talk with Casey to try and engage her. They are friends, so this may work. The two huddle together but don't seem to be doing anything constructive. That's OK for now.

After class I take Casey to the guidance counselor. She comes along willingly. Wanting to talk with her parents, I call the phone number on file, but it is no longer in use. The guidance counselor has the same problem. We never do learn what happened with the surgery because the following week, Casey and her family move away. No one seems to know anything about the family. It's rare to find out what happens to kids like Casey. Praying is the only thing.

On a happy note, the students improvise to create stage makeup. They find food coloring in the science cabinet. I warn them that this coloring may stay on for days, but they don't care. They're having fun. They also use some of my fresh carnation flowers. Not only do they pinch off leaves to smudge the green pigment onto their faces, but they do the same with the red carnations. Love their clever ideas!

Matthew 6:34 ...Do not worry about tomorrow, for tomorrow will worry about itself. Each day has enough trouble of its own.

Lord, help kids like Casey. Please forgive me that I didn't understand her, and forgive me that I didn't realize how bad things were for her. Give me understanding for the next student like Casey.

A Gift in Her Purse

One day John teases Mary, "What did you do to your hair?"

She replies hatefully, "You think I like you? You make me sick." In the old days, we thought this meant John had a crush on Mary but didn't know how to express his real feelings.

As a teenager my mother once told a boy that she wouldn't date him if he were the last boy on earth. She married him 45 years later. They were both 61. So when they were kids, did she really like him?

In middle school Rob likes Shelly, and she likes him. One day at lunch he holds the door open for her to pass through, but when she gets to the doorway, he slams it in her face. Strange doings. Another time as my class is coming in after lunch, Rob tells Shelly he has put a gift in her purse. As she hesitates, he smiles and tells her, "Go ahead, you'll like it." She doesn't like it. Her shrill scream is heard all over the building. And the class shrieks and laughs.

Rob has put six cockroaches in her purse. When she opens her purse, the roaches crawl nervously around and onto her hands. Right along with the kids, I am gagging in repulsion at the vile roach nest in her purse. We flail and bump into each other as we stomp the nasty things. How Rob managed to capture them and get them into her purse is still a mystery. A prank? Bullying? Yes, cruelty. Laughter is the natural response to such pranks. But I quickly turn the focus on

Shelly, shocked and traumatized not only by fear of roaches but by Rob's behavior. Calling Rob aside, I address the meanness.

On the bus one morning, Alan greets his classmates by offering a handshake. When they return the gesture, they feel sudden excruciating pain and draw back blood. A gift of friendship turns into an attack. He has transformed his hand into a weapon of masking tape loaded with thumbtacks. One shake of his hand and the tacks punch holes into his classmates' skin. When Principal Green asks why he has done this, Alan answers that it's just a joke. That week the principal requires every teacher in the entire school to cover a lesson on bullying. She adds, "And teach a lesson on bullying each month."

While Alan is suspended from school, my students and I discuss an article from the state newspaper on bullying. The takeaway I want for them is twofold. They must tell a parent or teacher when they are bullied, and they must report any bullying they see. The article thoroughly describes many types of bullying, some that might seem harmless on the surface. Laughter during mean behavior does not make the bully a funny guy, and those standing by and watching while someone is bullied are not innocent.

As the lesson unfolds, my students open up with their own stories. I learn that there is an unbelievable amount of bullying going on. Candice tells how Alan scraped the thumbtacks down her arm. Pushing up her sleeve, she reveals the long, deep scratches he made. With relief in her voice, she says, "I'm glad somebody finally told on Alan. I was afraid to tell my parents because people might be angry with me. My family and Alan's family are friends."

Matthew 7:12 ...Do to others as you would have them do to you.

Lord, protect my students from bullies. Change the faulty thinking of those who make light of bullying. These kids are all your children, even the bullies. Give me wisdom to teach the right things and fill my heart with love for each one.

Have a Heart

Julie drops by school one afternoon and is very upset. Students are ridiculing her daughter Rachael in 7th grade. Up until recently Rachael has been happier than ever in school this year, but kids are now being cruel. Julie describes numerous accounts of this. She will not name names. This cruelty in my students shocks me. I apologize and assure Julie that I will handle this. I have not observed any of this behavior toward Rachael. Usually a compassionate student comes and tells us about these things. But wily and sneaky kids choose a time when no one is around to hear or see.

Julie says Rachael will be out of school on Monday, so that would be a good time to talk with my classes. By the time Julie leaves, I am livid about my students' behavior. How can they do this to such a sweet, kind girl? My strongest requirement is for us to treat each other with respect, teacher and students alike. When I intervene in a conflict, I say, "We treat each other with respect. Always. Everywhere. I expect this from all of you."

On Monday I am prepared to let the students see my disappointment and sadness. I won't show my anger. If I do that, they will become angry. I begin, "Class, I need to talk with you about something very serious. It's about disrespecting a fellow student. A kind, hardworking student. Remember, we treat each other with respect."

My eyes tear up as I continue my sermon, "I look at each of you and see outstanding students, very brilliant people. I see top athletes. You're beautiful inside and out. Rachael is, too. Inside and out. But let me tell you, you may have all this today and suddenly lose it in the blink of an eye. You could have an accident and then no longer have these extraordinary talents and skills. You might be in a wheelchair. You might have a disability just like Rachael. How would you want people to treat you then?

"I couldn't be more disappointed in those of you who did this. I know most of you are not involved in this. It is only a few. If I get hold of the names of those of you who did this horrible thing, you will not get away with it, and you'll be very sorry. The depth of your cruelty is astonishing. I'm talking only to those who did this. And I apologize to those of you innocent students who have to listen to this." I stop and sweep my eyes around the room to look at each face. A handful of heads are down. Are these the ones? Are they feeling remorse for their behavior?

You see, Rachael was born with a severe birth defect. One teacher works with her throughout the day to help her with every-thing, including changing classes and using the restroom. A week later her mom Julie drops by my room to thank me. She is relieved that Rachael's classmates are being nice to her and tells me Ali and Denise apologized to Rachael with lots of tears and remorse. I already know this. Ali and Denise came to me after school on the day I talked to the class. They sobbed uncontrollably and apologized even to me for their meanness. Contrite hearts. As the Psalmist says, "You will not reject a broken and repentant heart, O God."

Mark 12:30-31 "Love the Lord your God with all your heart and with all your soul and with all your mind and with all your strength. ...Love your neighbor as yourself."

Lord, give me discernment to know when my students are being cruel to each other. Show me how to teach them to reach out with kindness to those who are hurting, lonely or different from them.

Fast Technology

In 2020 during the COVID pandemic, teachers had to teach by Zoom. Not the best word for a FaceTime lesson. Dictionary.com defines "zoom" as "to move or travel very quickly." Some dedicated teachers retired or quit because of Zoom teaching. Even young, inspired teachers found this a huge challenge. In 2000 we also had Zoom, but it was not the same thing.

Gladys and I are enjoying working in a new building. What a great perk to work in such a modern facility! We have new everything, including smart boards, another big challenge for us teachers who grew up in the Stone Age. But also updated for our pleasure are toilets. During our planning time we head straight to the restroom. Teachers are not allowed to leave students for any reason, so we are near death by the time our 10:30 break comes.

Gladys scurries into my classroom with alarm on her face. "Dear mercy, you won't believe these new toilets. When I went to flush, such a noise burst out that I fell back into the door. The water sprayed all over the toilet seat and the floor. I never saw anything like it. And even from four feet away, the water zoomed out and sprayed all over me. My good shoes are wet. Just look at the water on them. I'm not sure my clothes are clean now." Water moving very quickly.

"Sounds like they installed an airplane toilet," I laugh.

"Well I wouldn't know anything about that," she replies. "But you better be on the lookout for what these ole' boys are doing now.

I caught three of them holding a boy over the toilet upside down by his feet. I like to have killed all of 'em. The very idea of putting somebody's head down in a toilet and letting that dirty water wash over him, his face, eyes, mouth and all. They were flushing and dipping his head up and down. That can't be sanitary."

A week later at morning bathroom break, I notice that Joe doesn't go to the restroom with the other boys. I tell him he ought to go because he won't get another chance until lunchtime. He says no, he doesn't have to go. This happens several days in a row. He finally tells me that the boys are giving him a swirly. Leaving him in the classroom, I walk to the boys' restroom and stand outside. I hear all manner of horse play. There is loud laughter. "Stop! Stop!" a boy yells. A toilet is flushing over and over.

I hate to do this. It goes against every fiber of my being. But I feel I have no choice. I take a deep breath and brace myself. First I shout, "Teacher coming into the restroom!" As I storm in, I start with my theatrical fighting voice, "Get out of here! Now! Every last one of you!" And louder I boom out, "Get out! Get out! Do you hear me?" Two boys dive from the stall and duck their heads in guilt. I know them. Butch and Cade.

They are followed by a very small 6th grade boy who looks sheepish. "Come on," I say to the younger one. "I'll take care of this." Leaving a wide distance between us, he follows me out into the hall. After that, I don't let my student Joe go until the others return from the restroom. Now each day at break time, I stand much too close to the boys' restroom door so they can't try anything.

Deuteronomy 23:12 Designate a place outside the camp where you can go to relieve yourself.

Lord, help! All this new technology is sometimes too much. Maybe the old ways of the Hebrew children in the Bible were better.

Anger from a Deep Place

High school students are tough with us and with each other. At this high school I had the pleasure of teaching some of the finest 10th graders ever. They were not so tough and could get along with most anybody. That said, I had the worst teaching experience of my life at this school.

I am standing on my "spot," which is a place that signals students to stop what they are doing and pay full attention. Angus always pushes the boundaries. As I introduce Shakespeare's Julius Caesar, he gets up and stands beside his seat in the middle row at the back. He swaggers along the back wall to the pencil sharpener. (We didn't have laptops in those days.) I wait as he purposely bumps into his classmates. They don't react and remain very still.

Angus is not a student to confront in class. When our eyes meet, I raise my brows but continue with my lesson. He cranks that pencil sharpener a hundred times. I stop talking. Dead silence. Thankfully he finally stops but comes back toward the front. I step aside as I see that he is coming down the aisle closest to me. He leans down nose to nose with Shawn, who is directly in front of me. Angus growls at Shawn, "What are you lookin' at?"

Half Angus's size, Shawn draws his hands to his face and says softly, "Nothin."

Suddenly with no provocation, Angus sends several fast, hard punches into the side of Shawn's head. Blood flies. Shawn crashes, desk and all, to the floor. No one reacts. This should have knocked Shawn unconscious. Angus starts punching again. I yell, "Pull them apart!" No one moves a muscle. I run to press the panic button on the wall next to the door. Yes, we have a panic button. Angus relents, and in seconds, four security guards are jogging up the hall to my room. Angus and Shawn are taken by separate guards; Angus to the office and Shawn to the hospital. Later when I ask the class why no one tried to help Shawn, they say Angus and his friends would retaliate.

Shawn's grandparents press charges. I am asked numerous times to write a deposition of the incident. After writing the deposition a third time, I figure out I can use my computer and simply resend the deposition when they continue to ask for it. I never did understand why they kept asking me to write another deposition.

Plenty of kids like Angus live in poverty and abuse and somehow get out into the world and succeed. Then there are those who have been severely abandoned, physically abused, and neglected, with no anchor in their lives. They often turn to violent crime, and it starts early in life. They have a mean spirit and no hope for them except Jesus. Getting Angus to Jesus is a monumental challenge.

I have a relative who got into drugs and went to prison for it. He somehow landed in a worship service in prison where men were crying out and shouting to Jesus to save them. Speaking with his mom on the phone from prison, he told her he never wanted to go in there again. He called it the scary place. Maybe Angus needs the scary place.

Later in a conference, Angus's dad says that the previous year Angus broke both his arms and was out of school most of that year. He added that Angus killed someone in self-defense. I learned a few years later that he went to prison for murder.

Isaiah 41:10 So do not fear, for I am with you; be not dismayed, for I am your God. I will strengthen you and help you; I will uphold you with my righteous right hand.

Lord, you are our help. We are sometimes put in situations that are dangerous. Thank you for bringing us through. Help the helpless. Stop the violence, the shooting and killing. But also please help those who are angry and troubled. Manifest yourself to these kids. Stay their hands from violence.

Conference Puzzles

Hardly any profession besides teaching offers so many mind puzzles. Even at teacher training conferences, there are puzzles such as arranging travel, and a shared room in a decent hotel, all on a teacher allowance. We do get one free meal a day. Teachers living the high life.

One of the puzzles of being a teacher is that my looks apparently don't match the way a teacher should look. My colleague Lloyd once expressed doubt about my ability to teach. He remarked to my friend Laura, "She can teach? Really? I'm surprised." More puzzling is that Laura came back and told me this. I could have gone forever without that knowledge.

At a conference called Dynamic Lesson Plans, I am accompanied by several young and excellent teachers. In the first session the instructor administers a computer literacy test. Afterward we grade each other's tests. Frank grades mine and scowls, "I think something's wrong here. You only missed one." I reply, "Yes, I have become pretty proficient on the computer. I have taken several computer classes at the community college." He answers, "I can't believe it." He was not joking.

The moral of this story is that even though a person may not look intelligent, they may actually be intelligent. After all, Albert Einstein was a theoretical physicist who was awarded the 1921

Nobel Prize in physics. A genius. But when he started school, the teacher told his father he was too dumb to learn.

Another time at the Rigor and Relevance conference, there is the puzzling van mix-up. When the conference ends, my friend Kate and I offer to hike across the huge parking lot to fetch our van. The others gather outside the hotel lobby and wait for us to pick them up. As Kate and I jump into the van, I pant, "These seats are blue! We came in a van with red seats." Kate shakes her head and asks, "So you think this is not our van? Do you really remember red seats?" The van cranks, and we drive to pick up our fellow teachers.

As soon as Jane climbs aboard, she can't find the coat she'd left in the van. We weigh all the reasons why the coat isn't there. It was stolen, Jane left it in the motel or packed it in her suitcase. I again tell them, "I'm sure we're in the wrong van." They exchange glances of disbelief. I dig around in the glove compartment for the registration. The van is clearly not from our town. We fret as we drive back to get our own van. Our key works for both vans.

That Monday on the hall bulletin board is a photo of Kate and me in the wrong van and a caption that reads, Theft 101.

Psalm 126:2 Our mouths were filled with laughter, our tongues with songs of joy.

Lord, you bring joyful moments into our lives each day. Show us how to focus on them. Teach us to bring humor into our lives, especially in our work.

Salesman

At the end of a year, teachers always have to collect students' out-standing debt. The office keeps account of this. There's a fee if a student damages or loses a book, and students must turn in all money collected from fundraisers such as sales of magazines, candy, fruit, jars of spices, etc. Sam has not turned in his $50 for the candy sale.

Let me explain. Each year a company comes to the school to put on a fundraising event. They do a hard sell. We teachers participate at their urging. In the first vignette of this book, I describe how my teammates and I helped. The company dressed us in velcro suits. The motivational performance consisted of teachers slamming ourselves into a velcro wall.

By now, each student volunteer has sold a cardboard case of fifty nut and chocolate candy bars. It has slipped my mind that Sam did not bring in his money. And on the last day of school he was absent. I check my receipt book. Nothing. The office has a list of outstanding debt, and Sam's name is on it. His parents must pay.

Sam is a likeable and sometimes hard-working 7th grader. He is such a good dancer that when we do poetry presentations, he likes to include a dance number. He sometimes even dances his way into and out of the classroom. I discover too late that he only cuts loose in a familiar, comfortable group. I once persuaded him to get up in the gym at the beginning of a pep rally to show off his dance moves. Our principal gave permission. Here's what happened.

Sam selects the song "The Cha Cha Slide," and I provide the boom box. When it is time for Sam to get up and dance, he bounces right out in front of a gym full of wild middle schoolers and flashes his megawatt smile. I punch the button for his Cha Cha Slide music, and the bleachers start swaying right away.

Sam scans the audience full of faces and sees his buddies Shawn and Cliff laughing and jeering at him. He freezes in place. I hurry to him with words of support and gently nudge him forward. With a look of full terror, he stares me square in the eyes and says, "I can't do this." With hands on his hips, he steps nervously from side to side with doubt and disappointment for giving up. He rushes back to his seat and buries his head low in humiliation. I blame myself for this. I clearly misjudged his ease in front of an audience. Did I miss important cues?

Back to the end of school and Sam's candy money. School was out two days ago, so it's really the last teacher "work day" as we call them. Why those days are called "work days" baffles me. Every school day is a work day.

Anyway, Sam and his mom come to my classroom to visit. His mom is just as engaging as Sam, with the same beautiful smile. She explains that she has just paid the candy money in the office but wants to say goodbye and thank me for the wonderful year Sam has enjoyed in my class. I look at Sam and tell him how proud I am that he sold all fifty candy bars. His mother frowns at him, "He didn't sell any candy bars!" I'm thinking maybe his mom sold them.

Sam lowers his head and mumbles, "I ate 'em all."

Galatians 6:9 Let us not become weary in doing good, for at the proper time we will reap a harvest if we do not give up.

Lord, bless Sam and his mom. Bless his mom for teaching him to make things right in the end. May Sam never do anything so bad that it cannot be made right.

Are You That One?

Exasperated at student apathy, I complain to Principal Amy that the students don't want to learn. Amy retorts, "You've got to make them want to learn. You have to pull magic tricks out of your hat." Some days that seems impossible.

On the fourth week of school, parent Jean Wise calls me. She complains that I am punishing all the kids in the class because of the misbehavior of one. A couple of ticks of the clock go by before I grasp what Jean is talking about. She is upset about my incentive system, which helps me engage my students in a positive manner. The principal has given me permission to use this. I explain my system to Mrs. Wise. Here it is in brief.

The class has an opportunity to earn sixty points toward a snack and board game hour at the end of each month. They bring their own snacks, and extra in case a classmate forgets. At the beginning of each year, I get the class to create a list of actions that will earn them points. I post these behaviors on the wall, and we list the number of points each is worth. For example, if a guest or the principal comes into the classroom and the students are very polite, they earn three points.

We invented one rule out of necessity—they may not ask for points. Students were constantly whining, "You should give us points for that!" It got out of hand. Now if they ask for points, they lose three points. If they engage in a riotous free-for-all, they lose all their points and have to start over. I didn't share this part with Jean Wise, but what I do is engineer the points to come out so that the class always earns a snack and board game hour at the end of each month. I do this by spontaneously awarding them points for a behavior I think is extraordinary, whether it's the class or an individual student.

As far as getting students to cooperate, I'm thinking the new teacher Pat Blake might be very good at classroom management. She has been a police officer. We look forward to her help with student behavior. Maybe not. It turns out maybe she needs to learn our ways. Pat struggles from the first day. Principal Amy comes to my room one day and asks me whether I think Pat is doing a good job. I see how Pat interacts with the students, and she seems to be doing fine. I haven't gotten any complaints from the students. But being asked to critique a fellow teacher feels strange.

One day at lunch my student Greg tells me, "Ms. Blake grabbed John in a head lock and threw him to the floor." I take this news to Principal Amy who tells me she is getting complaints from students and parents. Ms. Blake has slapped a student and thrown a chair across the room at another. Before long she leaves, and a substitute is in her room. What follows in that classroom is a year of chaos. Some students are still suffering from the trauma of Ms. Blake, while others really liked her and feel it is unfair that she was fired. The substitute teacher has to deal with this fallout.

I get a new set of students in January. Their first assignment is to write in a journal about themselves. Tom gazes up at me and asks, "Didn't you use to be a policeman?" I am suddenly seized with the notion that this information could work for me. So without telling a lie, I look at Tom sternly and state, "We're not going to talk about this. The subject is off limits."

Students are overly polite in my room after that. Word gets around in the gossip pool that I am the mean policeman, and that I will throw them into a head lock if they don't follow the rules. I get new student, Morris, in February. I overhear Tom whisper to Morris, "She's mean. You better do what she says, or she'll karate slam you."

Proverbs 14:8 The wisdom of the prudent is to give thought to their ways.

Lord, teach me better ways to get my students to cooperate. Help me to give thought to my ways. Teach me to be firm but kind.

They Really Left Me

In a K-8 school, it is refreshing to see very young children. Although I teach 6th and 7th graders, it makes my day when the little ones call out a greeting to me. One of those is Cam, a wide-eyed 1st grader. To look at him is to adore this sweet child. His teacher Amber tells me a story about him.

Amber is on bus duty after school. She stands and waits about twenty minutes as bus after bus fills with kids and drives away. And there stands Cam. She asks him, "Did you miss the bus?" He answers that nobody is at his house. "Wait a minute," she says. "You missed the bus? And nobody is at your house?" To get the full story, she coaxes words from Cam. "So someone is coming in a car to pick you up?"

With no emotion Cam explains, "They ain't comin. Nobody's comin. When I went to the bus this morning, Mama told me when I get back won't nobody be there. She said they were leavin me behind. They all left."

"So who is picking you up?" Amber probes again with great patience. This roundabout way with words is the nature of little children. Cam is impatient. "I told you. They left. They ain't comin' back."

Amber speaks softly, "Let's go to the office and see if we can get you home." As they walk hand in hand up the long walkway, Cam repeats over and over, "Nobody's comin." By this time Amber is repressing a chuckle and thinking what a vivid imagination Cam has. She leads Cam to guidance counselor Della Davis and explains what is happening.

Ms. Davis calls his home phone. It is disconnected. "I think we better put Cam in my car and take him home," she states with worry.

After 12 miles of rough twists on a country road, they drive up a bumpy cow path. Della must slow down to keep from damaging the suspension of the car. They see a dilapidated mobile home surrounded by tall weeds. Almost before the car stops, Cam bolts around to the back of the house and calls his dog. "Mac! Mac!" he yells. Amber and Della follow Cam to make sure he is safe. He won't stop calling Mac's name. The women look at each other with pained expressions.

Amber whispers, "We're gonna step on a snake back here in this tall grass. I don't think this grass has been cut all season. I never knew that child was living like this. He seems fine. Has friends. Smiles and laughs."

When they catch up to Cam, he is crying. Tears leak from his eyes and wet the front of his shirt. They can barely hear him speak. "They even took my dog. He was my Christmas dog Grandma gave me. I did everything for him. I fed him, ran him and he slept in my bed with me. I got fleas last summer, but they put some flea powder on us. Me and Macaroni. That's his real name." Cam cries in waves. Coming up beside him, Amber gently puts her arm around his shoulders. He buries his head in her arms and sobs in great heaves.

As they walk back to the car, a dog barks in the distance. "Mac! It's Mac!" Cam yells. He and the dog run toward each other. "Hey Macaroni! I love you!" Cam cries anew.

Della peers into the windows at the empty living space. "They've really moved," she says, her eyes filling with tears. "I've never seen anything this bad."

Kissing and hugging his dog, Cam chokes on his words, "They really left me."

Matthew 19:14 Jesus said, "Let the little children come to me, and do not hinder them, for the kingdom of heaven belongs to such as these."

Lord, you know where Cam is today. He is now a grown man and surely scarred by this abandonment. Make strength from his scars. Make him a mighty man of God.

All in a Day

Everyone should teach in a dilapidated school, just once. One that is 110 years old. In 2007, soon-to-be President Obama, during his presidential campaign, visited my hometown. He said he hoped to save our school district, which was in the area that became nationally known as the Corridor of Shame. In one school we had to dodge holes in the wood stairs, and the ceiling plaster hit us in the head as it often crashed and fell. The school was built in 1896, my great-grandmother's era.

My first year of teaching, I find myself in such a school but am just thankful to be teaching. Supplies are short. We have to buy our own paper. The roof leaks when it rains hard, and on these days you might see several buckets in classrooms. Students don't even notice. The ceiling is so high that by the time a drop of water hits the bucket, it splashes on anyone sitting nearby. This is not a problem until a hard rain makes the splashes beat like seconds on a loud clock.

At lunch I am on hall duty. Principal Zach is making his rounds and stops to point out something on the floor. He says, "Do you see that?" I turn to see a tiny mouse about the size of a 10-year-old's thumb. It limps along the baseboard. I cringe and reply, "I can't believe this place has rats!" Mr. Zach looks at me with a matter-of-fact expression, "Ma'am, I've seen rats the size of a large cat in this building. I once had to shoot one with my pistol."

I frown hard at him and consider whether to ask him if he actually carries a gun at school. This is long before we ever had any school shootings. I decide not to say anything, his being the boss and all. Instead, I raise my eyebrows in reply. He continues, "That mouse is nothing. Just stomp it!"

Stomp on a mouse? I've bravely smashed many large roaches and spiders, but the vision I now have is a bloody mess all over my shoes, and this does not make me brave. Anyway, I don't crush mammals. Without another word, Mr. Zach nods at me to go ahead. I want to be tough and accomplish this deed for my boss. The first week at our opening teacher orientation, he talked to us at great length about being stern with the students. I remember his exact words were, "If you're afraid, you need to go home and find something else to do." I did that the following year.

But back to the menacing mouse. I'm determined to be tough. With my face turned away, my eyes and mouth tightly scrunched up, I put my toe on the mouse with a steady, gentle pressure. The little critter wriggles loose and continues to lippity-lip along the baseboard again. For some reason it avoids the floor itself. Mr. Zach moves ahead of me and steps on the mouse just enough to kill it without drawing blood. Not his first rodent kill. With a deep, shaky inhale, I continue my hall duty.

I have locked my classroom door but have not yet learned that students have ways of breaking in. While walking up the hall, I hear a ruckus breaking out in my room. As I near, I see Ken and Stacy fighting with a broomstick. Each one tugs and jerks the stick in an attempt to take the other one down. I open the door quickly and bark, "What's going on here?" This distraction gives the larger Stacy an advantage, and he wrestles the broomstick away from Ken.

Stacy then turns on me with the stick raised above his head and snarls, "If you won't the way you was, I'd hit you with this broomstick!" The way I was, was seven months pregnant with my daughter.

By now Principal Zach hears the raised voices and runs into the room. He quickly grabs the broomstick and escorts the now-frightened boys to the office. I will later have to write a detailed account of the incident.

I can't bring myself to eat a heavy school lunch today. Just a ginger ale and a pack of nab crackers. All in a day's work.

Hebrews 13:6 …The Lord is my helper; I will not be afraid. What can man do to me?

Lord, you know the fear we teachers feel in the midst of threats and violent fights. I pray for the safety of those teachers who are in a bunker every day, for the students who are victims of violence, and for the kids who feel compelled to solve disagreements with violence.

Book on Your Head

Fire drills often frighten little kids. My own 1st grade teacher Miss Cutter traumatized me when she announced after a fire drill that Judy and Alice had burned up in the fire. We didn't understand. They were both sitting right in front of us. Miss Cutter dragged her words slowly along in anger, "And that's what will happen to YOU if you STAY in the classroom as Judy and Alice did." I still remember looking across the table at Judy and Alice with confusion and wonder. They burned up? It took me a long time to decipher the truth.

In the spring, we have tornado drills. We are reading Romeo and Juliet in my 9th grade English class, when the tornado alarm suddenly makes its shrill blast. I nearly jump out of my skin. I hate it when we have a drill just when the lesson is getting good. The intercom alerts us to take a book and get into the hall immediately. As usual the students don't take it seriously.

Soon after we get into the hall, Principal George announces that a tornado has been spotted in our area. In the hall we prepare for the worst. Facing the wall, we crouch down on our knees and put books on our heads as a shield. The students cannot seem to hush. Suddenly we hear the familiar train sound followed by a huge scraping and popping noise. My heart lunges. I look up to see genuinely frightened teenagers. Though full of dread, I force myself to be calm and speak evenly, "I think the tornado has hit the school. If you're a praying person, now would be a good time to pray."

One of my tough boys, Jay, tries to hide his tears. I assure him, "We'll get through this." Sheila and Denise jump up to run, and in the den of noisy panic, I catch each by the arm and shout, "It's safer here. Things outside like trees and other heavy objects will be flying, and you don't want to be in that."

"I've got to call my mom!" Denise cries out.

Sheila weeps, "I have to get my baby sister from the daycare."

"You cannot go. You're safer here. Get back on the floor," I command. I'm struggling to conquer my own fear.

We hunker down and wait. Suddenly it becomes very quiet. The tornado has moved on. Thank God. But it has ripped off the gym roof. Students and teachers alike are in shock as we walk outside and see the damage. For days PE classes are on the football field. The teacher parking lot is littered with splintered lumber and gnarled aluminum, so we have to park along a side road. Each day students have to see the tornado damage.

As I'm leaving school that day, I look over at the huge amount of repair work to be done and admire the people who know how to rebuild this. I hear voices coming from the debris. It's not men's voices. Not intending to walk too close to the piles, I head in the direction of the sounds. I realize it's two teenagers, a girl and a boy. Oh dear. I call out to them, "You two all right in there?"

They answer right away, "We got a dog trapped in here. We heard him whining. Trying to get him out. But we're trapped. Can't find a way out."

I answer, "Be still and wait for the fire truck and EMS. Don't move! I'm dialing 911."

"We got the dog!" they yell back happily. Merciful Father, will they ever learn? Miraculously the kids are safely rescued, along with a beautiful chocolate labrador retriever. Guess that dog wanted to hunt.

Psalm 107:28-29 Then they cried out to the Lord in their trouble, and he brought them out of their distress. He stilled the storm to a whisper.

Lord, we are so often faced with frightening situations. We are sometimes scared even when there is nothing to fear. Show us how to trust you completely. Thank you for always being near.

She Inspires

Students of all ages fascinate and inspire me. Keeley is one of those. An imposing 7th grader, she is not liked much by the other students. She often verbally spars with them and irritates them. Some 7th graders struggle with this kind of aggressive debate. Keeley is gifted and has clever ideas to make the lesson more exciting. And I listen. Allowing her to use her ideas is a good challenge. This year, besides my English classes, I have two science classes. Keeley likes science and tells me she wants to make silly putty.

Sometimes Keeley stirs up her classmates in a myriad of clever ways such as addressing them during my teaching. Once she challenged me by shouting, "That's not what the poet meant!" She's expressing her opinion. Expression is fine, but not rudeness. That's why it is a good plan to have her actually teach the class. She can demonstrate how to make silly putty. I give her a rubric which includes five things: 1) engage class interest, 2) show the materials to be used, 3) go through the steps, 4) ask the class at least three questions, and 5) have the class summarize.

This proves to be demanding for her. When she arrives at school on the day of her presentation, she tells me she's only had two hours of sleep. Oh dear. But she is very organized, and her voice is strong and clear. Her work is flawless. The class enjoys it, and they even applaud at the end, which pleases her. But there is one snag that frustrates her. In the middle of her demonstration, the students ask too many questions. They are curious about the procedure. In reaction Keeley becomes demanding and rude, and the class responds by being rowdy and rude right back at her.

She orders them several times to "shut up," and I urge her to use the words "please hush" instead. With her face reddening, she looks my way for help. Clay and Hank throw spitballs at her. It's time to put a halt to this.

I send Clay to the library for a book of science experiments, and make Hank take one of my "wild goose chase" notes to the office secretary. Those two will miss the fun part of the silly putty. I offer the rest of the class an incentive, "If you are quiet and respectful, you may earn 10 incentive points toward your end-of-month snack and board game hour." Do they deserve an incentive? Maybe not, but neither is this the time for a sermonette, and I don't believe in punishing the entire class.

This experience earns Keeley some respect from her classmates. Sadly, Keeley has an angry, abusive father. Principal Lena has told us teachers to keep our room doors locked, and if he comes to the door, we are not to let him in. Hopefully he won't insist. One day her dad shows up at my room door during a class. Instead of letting him in, I step outside the room to talk. He is insistent to see her and peeks through the door glass to try and find her in the room. I doubt that he signed in at the office first. I tell him Keeley doesn't take this class now. He gets a little huffy with me and raises his voice, "You can't keep me from seeing my child."

Concerned about what he might do, I am polite. I keep my voice soft. I reply, "I'm only saying she is in someone else's class now." I won't tell him that Keeley is in the gym.

"Where is she then?" he demands.

"Sir, you'll have to go to the office and ask the principal. I don't know," I say steadily.

"You teachers know the kids' schedules," he loudly persists with a menacing frown.

About that time my teammate walks over to us. "Sir, we are not allowed to give out that information." At that he storms off.

Later when I see Keeley at lunch, I tell her that her dad stopped in to see her. She studies my face and replies, "He doesn't bother me." But I wonder.

Isaiah 30:21 Whether you turn to the right or to the left, your ears will hear a voice behind you saying, "This is the way; walk in it."

Lord, help me to balance the teaching of respect and incentives. Show me how to handle the various behaviors of my students in ways that show and teach them respect.

A Golden Book

Noble is a 7th grader who can do grade-level work, but he has other, more pressing responsibilities. Noble must help his mom. She is a single parent who goes to work about the time Noble gets home from school. He takes care of his two younger brothers every night. Mom gets home about the time the boys are waking up for their day.

When it comes to his school work, he is a last-minute doer. But he is strategic. He knows he must do enough work to pass 7th grade.

Four times a year, I assign book reports. Students do a presentation using my rubric. They enjoy the freedom to create wildly. About a week before the reports are due, I put them in cooperative learning groups where they can work the rubric and share ideas. I steer them. I notice that Noble doesn't have a book. He's playing in class.

Students like to wear a costume for their report. I have patched together a privacy curtain at the back of the room. Behind the curtain, they put hats, robes, rags or masks over their clothes, and they bring items such as face paint from home. Anne reads Harry Potter. She engages her audience by leaping from behind the curtain as evil Lord Voldemort. The class shrieks in fear and delight. She packs on so much face paint that she is green for four days. Vinny reads a book about football. Before I can stop him, he hurls a football across the room to his buddy, which takes "engage your audience" to cinema levels. I wonder how to ban such stunts in future assignments.

It is Noble's turn. He props his book on the podium and the class roars with laughter. Startled, I glance up from my notes to see a preschool Little Golden Book with a puppy on the cover. With a scowl I say, "Noble, are you pulling a scam?"

Noble begins, "You see, I was waiting on the bus this morning and when I saw it coming, I started out the door, but then my eye caught on my little brother's book and I quick grabbed it. I say Mrs. F always told us any grade is better than a zero. She says don't you dare come in here with nothing. Bring in something so you get a grade. So here it comes: *The Poky Little Puppy*. The author is Golden Books. What I liked about this book was…" Noble hesitates to think of a good answer. Gil calls out, "You like dogs!" Now the others are offering him answers, as if he's on the TV game show The Price Is Right, where the audience helps contestants by yelling out answers.

Noble answers Gil, "Yeah you know we fight dogs. I got a real pretty, brown pit bull. His coat is so shiny."

I interrupt here, "Noble, let's get on with your book report." I'm concerned that he'll begin bragging about dogfighting. Does he know it's illegal? According to the Humane Society, dogfighting is an inhumane blood sport in which dogs are bred and trained to fight. They are put in a pit to fight each other for spectator entertainment and profit.

Looking down at a borrowed rubric, Noble continues, "What I like about this book is the puppies 'cause I love dogs. The main character is the poky little puppy. His conflict is he tried to run with the big dogs, but he can't. The theme is about trying to do something you know you can't do. What I liked most about the book is that I don't get a zero."

At this the class again convulses with laughter. Noble finishes, "Here's my passage I picked to read to you: 'And down they went to see, roly-poly, pell-mell, tumble-bumble till they came to the green grass.'"

As I reflect, one thing is for sure. The class and I have been thoroughly entertained. As Noble stood at the podium today, he gave his best effort. He didn't have a choice.

I've told people this story about Noble many times over the years, and invariably they respond with, "I hope you gave him 100 for his effort!" They are disappointed when I answer that I gave him a 70. If I give Noble a high grade on this report, I send the message to the other students that you can choose any old book on any grade level and pull off a book report.

Those who don't teach cannot begin to understand the wise things we do for our students. And here is yet another of our 1,500 decisions in a day.

James 1:27 Religion that God our Father accepts as pure and faultless is this: to look after orphans and widows in their distress.

Lord, you send us such wonderful kids, likeable and kind.
In spite of their circumstances, they succeed.
Thank you so much, Lord. Praise you for such gifts.

Hello Again

Four boys—Jake, Theo, Arnie, and Wayne—are 8th graders in my first year of teaching. They cannot keep still. And they come as a package. I never know which one is doing what. One smashes ink into the seat of a classmate's desk and ruins her jeans. One steals six chalkboard erasers. Two days later, a school board member brings me six new erasers. Jake's dad is that board member. One of the boys brings a tiny tape recorder to school. I find it in his desk after school and play the tape. I hear my own voice loud and clear as I teach how to learn a list of intransitive verbs by singing them to the tune of "Twinkle Twinkle Little Star." In case you're curious, here it is:

Be, been, is, are, was, were, am,

Being, seem, feel, look, smell, taste, sound

English teachers today don't teach much grammar, and probably not intransitive verbs. Nobody much remembers parsing and diagramming sentences. None of the students I taught in my last 15 years had ever heard of the song "Twinkle Twinkle Little Star."

Nine years later I get a call from Wayne's mother that he's taking a class and needs the title of that grammar handbook we used in my class. We didn't have enough English textbooks to go around, so I taught from a paperback the parents bought. Though Wayne did not study much then, he realizes the importance of it now.

Fast forward some 20 years, and I see Arnie in the grocery store. We talk only briefly, and I don't mention any of his 8th grade shenanigans. A few weeks later his mom tells me that when Arnie saw me, he was shocked at how small I was. She laughed because he said, "Mom! Mrs. F used to be big!" The eyes of a child only see big adults.

I also have the opportunity of teaching Theo's child, Marty. One day I walk into my classroom to see Marty stealing money from my desk drawer. He has picked the lock. The money is for our field trip. I escort him to the office and leave him with Principal Moore. As I fill out the incident report, Mr. Moore leaves his office with Marty sitting alone. Marty sticks his head out the door and says to me, "Do you know who my dad is? He can have you fired." I tell him yes, I do know his dad and that I plan to visit his law office and tell him what happened.

Marty's dad, Theo, is very angry, so Marty is remorseful when he returns from his days of suspension. As the class leaves for lunch, Marty walks up to me sheepishly and says, "Hello again. I need to say something to you, Mrs. F. I apologize for what I did, stealing the money, and here's money to pay it back. And I apologize for saying to you who my dad is and how he could get you fired." I am surprised but gladly accept his apology. Marty knows his dad will check with me to see if he gave the apology properly. We get along fine after that.

**Luke 17:3 So watch yourselves.
If your brother sins, rebuke him,
and if he repents, forgive him.**

*Lord, I was angry with Marty. I never imagined that he could
give such an apology. Let me always be careful to have a
forgiving spirit and not hold on to my anger.*

Move Out

Rural areas in the south abound with snakes. My student Leah is helping me clean my classroom at the beginning of the school year. She looks behind the door for the broom. As she grabs it, she gasps at a baby copperhead. Venomous. The tiny thing is apparently sick because it is not trying to get away. The custodian surmises that the snake is sick from the strong cleaning fluid used in the school.

Surrounded by farms and fields, our campus sees quite a few snakes. One day Joan, our school receptionist, reaches under her desk to get her boots and finds a snake, calmly gazing at her. When she screams "Snake!" Principal Hayes calls one of the 12-year-old farmers in the hall, "Come quick, Grady!" The boy runs into the office. He looks at the snake a long minute, snatches it by the back of its head and carries it gingerly out to the woods behind the school. When he returns, Grady informs us that this was a king snake. At ease with his subject, he explains that when king snakes are around, there won't be any venomous snakes because the king snakes run them away or kill them. He adds that they kill them by constriction. That's why they're the kings! Grady beams at his knowledge.

Then there is the time my teammate Lily waits in line with her students under the awning between buildings. Something heavy falls from the awning onto her head, onto her shoulder and finally onto the paved walk. A fat snake. The kids assure her it's just a corn snake. When it hits the concrete walk, the sound of the splat is like the sound of dropping a 10-pound ham. The snake slithers unharmed into the bushes. Lily doesn't seem bothered by it. Such an amazing thing that most of the time snakes don't bite.

My granddad tells me the story of an incident that happened when he worked for the highway department in our tiny South Carolina town. He is assigned to lead a crew of workmen to repair a bridge. They ride in two trucks out to the bridge, which is on a secondary road. Rarely do we see any traffic on those roads. Before starting work, they stand around the area and survey their surroundings. When my granddad bends down to peer into the dark, concrete pipe under the bridge, it is crawling with snakes. He jumps back and says to the men, "We won't be working the bridge today, men! Someone's got to get all these water moccasins out. It won't be us." He laughs when he tells that.

My student Azalee lives in a shack with no windows or doors, just open rectangles with no glass. It's 1974. She misses eight days of school. I try to reach her parents, but there is no phone. The social worker drives out to her house to check on her. The family has moved. Eventually Azalee turns up at school again. When asked where she has been, she nonchalantly shares that snakes got so bad in her house, they had to move out. She shows no emotion, seems not to have experienced any fear. Her classmate Jackie asks her how many snakes got into her house. Azalee answers in monotone, "Maybe 50."

Have you ever seen a bunch of snakes snuggled up together in a ball? That's mating season and that means move out.

Jeremiah 1:8 "Do not be afraid of them, for I am with you and will rescue you," declares the Lord.

Lord, you have protected us so many times. Help children like Azalee. Provide a good home for all who need one.

Non Toxic

Growing up, I never liked science. In my day I had a couple of science teachers who called on students to read one boring paragraph after another. I dreaded my turn to read because I had a reading problem that consisted of stumble, stop, repeat. I worked twice as hard as my classmates in college to earn a degree in English. Teaching was no picnic for me either.

This year the school is short of a science teacher, so I fill in with my vast lack of science knowledge. Thankfully the modern science textbook contains exciting, detailed experiments with photos and not just words.

To teach water pollution, I draw aquifers on the board. I do this every year for each of my classes. Students get it when I use art and music. I am no artist, but I boldly sketch crude houses with plumbing and underground pipes. Below that, I make a squiggly flowing line for the aquifer. I explain, "Let's say you painted a chair. You pour some paint thinner into a jar to soak your brush and then clean it. You wash the rest of the paint thinner down the sink, and it flows through the underground pipes, into your septic tank and eventually into the aquifer."

I move my pointing stick along the route as I explain, "It runs down and down until it reaches your neighbor's well. What do you think just happened?" Chase replies, "You cleaned up the mess." Oh the rapturous laughter of teaching middle school.

In a lesson called Kitchen Science, we learn about toxins and non toxins. We are experimenting with nontoxic cleaning supplies. I have the students mix baking soda and water, and with a paper towel they scrub their desks. I tell them this cleaning supply will not harm their skin. Bucky asks whether he can drink it. I tell him, "If you swallow it, it will not hurt you, but..." Before I can say "don't swallow it," Bucky removes the spray mechanism and drinks from the bottle. He remarks, "It don't taste too bad. Good as toilet water." All this he says to ignite the class, and it works.

Our next lesson is about air pollution. When I assign presentations, I require students to turn in a written plan a week before they present. I talk with each student to make sure they have a workable plan. I don't want any surprises. But I discover too late that Chase did not turn in a plan. I forgot to make a list and check it twice.

It's Chase's turn to present. He climbs up on a table and stands there looking around. We look expectantly at him and at the gallon bucket he is carrying. Waiting. Waiting.

Finally he begins to explain what air pollution is and what it does to us and our environment. Suddenly without preface, he reaches into his bucket and pulls out a hefty fistful of dirt. With great joy and vigor, he tosses fistfuls of dusty peat moss up toward the ceiling. It falls everywhere. As it scatters down on us, we gasp and cough. Over and over he tosses the dirt up to the ceiling. Students yell, "Stop throwing it!" and "You threw dirt all over me!" He waits for the full effect and then concludes, "This is air pollution."

Technically, this is a valid experiment. The class and I are certainly suffering from poor air. We are breathing the nasty stuff. It's certainly pollution. Now I must figure out a grade for Chase. Thankfully, I have created a grading rubric, but I'm not happy that he has completed every item on the checklist. "Chase, you completed the assignment accurately," I cough and try to hide my disgust at the mess all over the floor, the desks, the ceiling and us. "Now go and get the broom and dustpan and clean up this pollution."

I need to be like Santa Claus, make a list and check it twice.

Isaiah 55:1 Come, all you who are thirsty; come to the waters.

Lord, teach us how to care for your land, air, and water.
Thank you for fresh water that flows into our homes.
Help those who must carry a bucket of water from a well.

Driving Miss Maisy

In the 1970s teachers do not suffer repercussions for giving a student a ride home from school. Sometimes a kid misses the bus, and sometimes a parent doesn't show up, so one of us teachers gives the child a ride home. It's a community thing.

What happened to me is embarrassing. As always in the afternoon, I pick up my 1st grade daughter, Mary Beth, at school. On this day I get home from work about 2:30 in the afternoon and soon fall fast asleep in my chair. When I awake, it is nearly 5 p.m. I am frantic. I call the school, and the principal tells me that Mary Beth has gone home with her teacher Mrs. Susan Crane.

I drive over to Susan's house, only three small-town blocks away. In my humiliation I apologize over and over again. But Susan is gracious. She assures me that she understands and tells me she enjoys Mary Beth. Susan has given her a snack and started her on homework assignments. I can only thank her and add that I owe her a favor. The only person who is indignant is little Mary Beth, who lambasts me in the car. She really gets to me when she says, "Mama, you forgot me."

In another case I am keeping 8th grader Carrin after school. I arrange ahead with her mom to tutor Carrin after school each day because she has missed a couple of weeks of school and needs to catch up. When our session is over, Carrin informs me that no one is able to pick her up. I offer her a ride home. It concerns me when

I let her out that there is no one home to greet her. She is a latchkey kid. But I was a latchkey kid, too, and often hitched rides from school with neighbors.

This brings me to the story of 12-year-old Maisy. With tears Maisy often talks to me about her dad, who goes back to Mexico occasionally to see her grandparents, whom he hopes to bring back to the U.S. She worries that when her dad goes, he may never be able to come back. She cries a lot about this. Maisy never tells me whether her parents are undocumented. I don't ask. She tells me her older teenage sister Marabel drives them to school every day and is a scary driver. Marabel doesn't have a driver's license.

I am driving along I-40 one Saturday morning and notice the car behind me weaving dangerously. Obviously a drunk driver. This goes on for maybe a mile until the driver settles into the left lane. Suddenly I am terrified. He is about to pass me on the left. He loudly blasts the horn half a dozen times, which startles me. I can't move over to the right any farther.

As the car comes up even with mine, the driver catches my attention by enthusiastically waving both arms. While trying to keep my car in the right lane, I strain to look at this crazy drunk. I exclaim aloud, "That's a very short person at the wheel." As it flashes by at 75 mph, I recognize Maisy, smiling, waving and weaving. Lord, help us. A million thoughts run through my head.

**Philippians 2:4 Each of you should look
not only to your own interests, but also
to the interests of others.**

*Lord, it is difficult to make good decisions about helping others.
It can get us into trouble in today's world. But I believe
helping others is always right. Guide me so that I'm not
afraid to help others when I am able.*

Are You Rich?

I enter the old, crumbling school building. The exterior of the building has just been painted, new windows installed, but the dark interior is still shabby. This school district is not rich. Our lesson today is Alice Walker's essay "In Search of Our Mothers' Gardens."

As we read the piece together, I have the students write down phrases that jump out at them, any phrase that makes them think. I assure them that there are no wrong answers. Most of them choose phrases about Walker's overworked mother with her long, never-ending days of standing. Lucy looks deeply into the piece. She likes the phrases "stories dying without conclusion" and "shabby house we were forced to live in." I coax the students to see that though Walker lived in poverty and faced racism, she has a positive message about perseverance and creativity.

Grady's dad is a corn and soybean farmer. He likes the line in the story, "Whatever she planted grew as if by magic." He tells us, "My dad can grow things like that. Like magic." I like to see my students involved in this type of thinking. Grady's eyes sparkle as he thinks about his dad's crops growing well. A future farmer.

Lucy's mind is laser focused on a different theme. She looks up at me and asks, "Are you rich?" That's all. My answer to her is honest. I say, "Lucy, if I were rich, I wouldn't have to work like I do. I'm not rich, but I'm very happy in my life. I feel rich. I'm rich in love, joy and peace." Lucy argues, "It's not fair for some people to have to work and others not to." I let that marinade.

Students ask where Alice Walker lives and is she still alive. Dave asks whether Walker ever found her mother's garden. Oh dear. Sophia is concerned that Walker's mother ran away from home and got married. I don't tell them that I did the same when I was 18 years old. Though I feel this piece is too difficult for them, I guide them through it. Bella is impressed with the line about the 100-year-old quilt made from rags. She says dreamily, "I can see the Crucifixion scene in my mind. Made of rags. I bet it's pretty."

We look at what Walker writes about this quilt. It's Harriet Powers's 1886 Bible Quilt, among the National Quilts in the Smithsonian Institution in Washington, D.C. I ask, "What do you think the author means by 'feeding the creative spirit?'" One class clown yells out, "Giving her food!" Dear Lord, will it never end? Lucy ponders this and says, "It's like a spirit that gets in you and it makes you creative. But you don't feed it food. I don't know what you feed it."

I explain that it's something creative we do to make us happy, such as playing a musical instrument or planting a garden of flowers, like Alice's mother did. This feeds the mind and soul, especially when a person lives in poverty. Lucy replies, "Like when you said you feel rich because you're happy."

Although they don't quite get Alice Walker's meaning, we are in a good place with this piece of literature. The mood and their focus is very satisfying. But suddenly, I notice a blue pickup truck rolling slowly across the grass toward my window. It looks as if it might hit the building. It stops right in front of the window, and a man jumps out with a basket. Grady gasps, "That's my Papa! Can

I go, Mrs. F?" What in the world? I know his dad, so I relinquish in frustration, "Yes, go ahead!"

The class is rapt at this bright new development. I open the window as Grady's dad walks up. When Grady reaches his dad, the two of them laugh at what's in the basket. Grady sticks his head through the open window and shouts, "These are my new huntin' dogs. Bird dogs. Papa just brought 'em in the truck." His face turns sad. "We had two but they dug out the pen and ran off down the road. An 18-wheeler hit 'em." He cheers up again, "But look here at these two!" He holds one of them up. "Ain't they pretty?"

And they are. His dad and I exchange a knowing smile about this happy disruption of a classroom of sweet, innocent kids who love their families, mostly work hard, and fill our hearts with all the meaning of life. A different kind of rich.

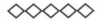

**James 2:5 Listen my dear brothers:
Has not God chosen those who are poor in the
eyes of the world to be rich in faith and
to inherit the kingdom he promised
those who love him?**

*Lord, help me not to be offended when a student asks me a
personal question. Give me a heart to look through the question
and into the probing mind of such students as Lucy.
Thank you for lavishing us with your love.*

Bibliography

Books:

Field Guide to North American Reptiles & Amphibians. New York: The Audubon Society. 1979

The Holy Bible, New International Version, Colorado Springs, CO: International Bible Society. 1984

Lowrey, Janette Sebring and Gustaf Tenggren. *Poky Little Puppy.* New York: Little Golden Books, Simon & Schuster. 1942

Walker, Alice. "In Search of Our Mothers' Gardens." *Macmillan Literature Series Introducing Literature.* New York: Glencoe Macmillan/McGraw-Hill. 1991

Websites:

Benson, Tom. "Brief History of Rockets." National Aeronautics and Space Administration. 13 May 2021 grc.nasa.gov

Bowers, Shelby. "South Carolina's Corridor of Shame." 19 April 2021. storymaps.arcgis.com

The Humane Society of the United States. Washington, D.C. 2021. humanesociety.org

"The National Quilt Collection." National Museum of American History. Smithsonian Institution. Washington, D.C. 1890. americanhistory.si.edu

Water Education Foundation. 2021. watereducation.org